MINESHAFT CANARIES

100 selected poems

By
Monte Akers

Dedication

To Madison, Harper, Knox, and Ariya

Table of Contents

Dedication 1

Introduction 3

About Poetry 4

Humor And Whimsy 10

Philosophy/World View 24

Religion..40

Love 45

Death 57

Family/Friends... 65

Politics And The Nation 71

Storytelling 81

History 95

Civil War.. 99

Closing 122

Introduction

At age 15, when I wrote a joke poem about my two best friends and me, I never dreamed that sixty years later I would have a book of my poetry published. In fact, the idea might have sent me into a spiral of adolescent despair about my future. Over the years, however, I wrote hundreds of poems, lyrics, and doggerel, and the facts that I've been married for 44 years, obtained a law degree, raised a family, practiced law for 44 years, and have nine other books published replaced all despair. I've had some of my lyrics turned into songs, received occasional compliments about a few, and decided that producing a small volume of the better rhymes was in order.

The poems in this book cover a range of topics, including whimsy, lost love, humor, death, religion, politics, and particularly American history. They are presented under such categories. I know better than to think these poems will have an audience beyond selected family and friends. Truth is, I would recoil in horror if someone sent me a collection of their poetry to read. Accordingly, please do not feel any obligation to comment, thank me, or firebomb my house. However, to those who will read them, please enjoy, chuckle, or scratch your head.

Monte Akers

December 31, 2025

About Poetry

Canaries

There's no longer much petition
for the poet's structured craft.
Poetry's the yellow bird in a cage
in mankind's coal mine shaft.

Don't Fistfight with A Poet

Don't fistfight with a poet,
even tho' he's such a nerd.
You may whip his ass with fists;
he may whip your ass with words.

His bumps and bruises all will heal,
as wherever you put a knife,
but a well-placed rhyme about you,
could haunt you all of your life.

Poets

Poets place their senses

on open public shelves,

dream life as it ought to be,

and sometimes kill themselves.

Trelawney's Fable

After Percy Bysshe Shelley drowned in 1822, his body was burned on a beach, and his friend, Edward Trelawney, retrieved and preserved what he thought was the poet's heart. It was almost certainly his liver, the most blood-gorged organ and the most resistant to fire.

Trelawney reached into the pyre,

the ocean poet's funeral fire,

to seize the heart, tho' charred, intact,

and give romance enduring fact.

And tho' the heart of Shelley beats

on in words, with Byron's, Keats',

t'was fable only could Trelawney give—

romance won't cause a liver to live.

Desolation Deified

Shelley to Mary, upon the death of their daughter, Clara, in 1817.

Find no dignity in grief beyond its gestation.

Ours is not others' lifeblood—the small
relation.

The snow's smothering of autumn, though
total, is brief.

There must follow a spring, and from
mourning, relief.

Do not claim a bell's pealing when it's meant
for us all,

nor the gleam of the cumulus when its shadows
befall.

Escape not to yourself, if the vessel is hollow,

nor to earlier yearnings, where I cannot follow.

Live now for our oneness, its life celebrate.

Cause not its dying, a death which predates

the time for my passing, which surely must
come,

which will be worth your mourning but will
leave you as one.

Rosetti

Oh Dante Rosetti, were those rhymes worth
what you've done,

disturbing poor Elizabeth, when her slumbers
just begun?

Grief can cause a man to do things beside
shedding tears,

but did you really have to dig her up? She's
been dead for seven years!

Maybe putting your unpublished works, all
poetry I believe,

into the casket with your dead wife was not the
way to grieve.

But having written words that rhyme, I sort of
understand—

some rhymes of mine should be covered up too,
perhaps by a cat in its sand.

It Isn't Art

I like to write poems about living,

the how, the what, and the which,

It isn't art,

or even smart.

I'm just a rhyming son of a bitch.

Poems I Have Written

I read more than four hundred poems
and copied over half.
Some of them were embarrassing.
Some of them made me laugh.
Some were clever, most were not.
In some I bared my all.
Some were carefully engineered.
Most were in childish scrawl.
You may wonder why I ever wrote
things copied here today,
but I bet you've had some twisted thoughts,
and you let them slip away.

I didn't.

In 1994, a collection of my poems was accepted by a small poetry-focused publishing house, after which the manuscript was prepared for publication. As a title, I selected the headings of two of the poems, "Civil War Battles I was In" and "Women I saw Naked," then hired a photographer who specialized in nudes and a professional model for an interesting photo shoot. Then, after the collection was finalized and an ISBN was acquired, communication with the publisher mysteriously stopped. After repeated attempts to find out why, I learned that he had died (it was truly a small publishing house), so the collection was never published. The following are the front and rear covers for that unpublished work.

Humor And Whimsy

Incredible

If I eat it, it must be edible.

If I tell the truth I am credible.

If food spoils it becomes inedible,

so I guess when I lie, I'm incredible.

Big Apple Weekend

Went to New York,

ate pizza with a fork,

marveled at the way they talk,

kept my money in my sock.

Saw a play on a stage,

saw some lions in a cage,

rode a taxi, paid a toll,

saw the 9/11 hole.

Watched the neon in Times Square

had a barber cut my hair,

saw some ships along a pier,

bought a t-shirt souvenir.

There were gay guys with a sign,

black ties and ball gowns in a line,

big fat Jewish guys with beards.

I was the only one not weird.

Dog Thoughts

I send you words; would they were arrows.

Arrows fly straight; words stray from the mark.

My heart is wide, but its message is narrow.

I try to converse, but I might as well bark.

Tribal Trouble

A hip hop floozie who was a Rapper ho*

rode a Brule* bull in the Crowdeo*.

She wasn't sweet Sue* and she wasn't Shy
Ann*.

She was Lakota* from Dakota*, from a he-
Mandan.*

Her daddy was a stud, a real Hunk Papa*,

but he wore a pink blanket, sort of a Chicka
shawl.*

He walked with a limp, had a bad Pa Knee*,

would sit for long spells in his Chair o kee*.

His toes froze bad, he had two Blackfeet*,

But he kept on wearing that pink Shawl neat*.

He was about half smart, sort of a Semi-know*,

but he didn't know his daughter was a Rapper ho*.

*Arapaho; Brule—a subtribe of the Teton Lakota; Crow; Sioux, or Lakota; Cheyenne; Sioux; A subdivision of a subtribe of the Lakota; a tribe of the great plains; Hunkpapa--one of the seven councils of the Lakota; Chickasaw; Pawnee; Cherokee; Piegan Blackfeet; Shawnee; Seminole; Arapaho

Ozmopolitan

Ducks are like goats, neither can whistle.

Both cook down to grease and gristle.

Men, like dogs, are guileless critters.

Women, like cats, cover shit with litter.

Children, like onions, add flavor, make you cry.

Your soul, like new color, comes out when you dye.

Nailed It

Menkauf said of papyrus
"Not nearly as good," he whined,
"as our storytelling tradition
which, for ages, has been just fine.

"We should rely on the teller of tales;
not draw words on a river leaf.
Mark my words; I know these things.
This idea will come to grief."

Benjaman scoffed at the railroad,
"How absurd can an idea be?
Nobody's going to lay steel and wood ties
from here to the distant sea.

"God intended we ride on a horse
or in wagons, such as that.
The day trains are more than a novelty,
is the day I'll eat my hat."

My father-in-law had a Ph.D.
in "hating" anything strange,
like rock and roll and brown folks,
or anything mistaken for change.

Toward Elvis and Martin Luther King
he made some unveiled threats,
about their being passing fancies
in a time we would all forget.

There's always been lots of geniuses
who throughout time have known
that whatever changes they dislike
Will be wrong for everyone.

Ducky and the Professor

Ducky and the Professor
were lost in a foggy haze
on the edge of the Sea of Sargassum,
at the end of the halcyon days.
So Ducky waxed poetic,
swore love would dam the flux,
but the Professor wouldn't buy it,
and just said "NO" to Ducks.

Then Ducky felt a lonesome
jangle in his jeans,
at the end of his Pater Noster,
in front of the Magdelines,
and it seemed so damned familiar,
substantial, sweet, and pure
that he moored it to his beegum
with chains of gossamer.

And the Professor let him do it,
never raised the slightest fuss,
was too busy planning history
and ways to champion us.
Now when he mentions Ducky,
he describes a one-man act,
which seems like the fact of the matter
but may be a matter of fact.

Sitting Here in the Third World War

Sitting here in the third world war,
nothing's changed; we're doing fine.
America has time to go underground,
time to dig, time to mine.
The nuclear cloud from the Middle East
won't come 'til the fall; that's weeks away.
The germ warfare plague from Africa
won't be here 'til Spring.
There's time to play.

The chemical blight the Europeans know
could take years to cross, the tide's so slow,
and it's the same with pollution from rotting flesh
that will wash in from Asia—our water's still fresh.
Shoot, all the fears about World War Three
were just radical panic; there's no reason to flee.
God favors America. We're safe and sound.
We'll live here forever, safe underground.

Mirror

It's the team our team is beating.

It's the new fast food we're eating.

It's the news the Web's reporting.

It's the politics, so distorting.

It's the pandemic that's infecting.

It's the same old face reflecting.

Don't Pet the Burning Dog

It's mighty tempting, I know.

It's so friendly and slow.

Its brown eyes are all aglow,

but don't pet the burning dog.

I know you think you'll help,

but you'll only make it yelp,

and you might yelp yourselp,

if you pet the burning dog.

Chorus:

> Didn't your mama teach you?
> Don't put your hand in a fire.
> Didn't her plan ever reach you?
> Be honest, grow old, retire.
> Sometimes during the game,
> something comes in from the fog
> that reduces good plans to shame,
> if you pet the burning dog.
>
> She's pretty and young.
> She must be on the run,
> and she thinks you're the one.
> But she's really a burning dog.
>
> For just a few thousand bucks,
> instead of expecting luck—
> invest in robotic ducks.
> Look out, it's a burning dog.
>
> This man will make you a star.
> He loves how you play your guitar.
> He's a music publishing Czar,
> or maybe he's a burning dog.
>
> But then sometimes all there is
> that has some flicker and some fizz
> on that long road to show biz,
> is a flammable, pettable dog.

Here's a Job for Alcohol.

With her, I felt on top of the world.

That's a mighty long way to fall.

Move over coffee;

here's a job for alcohol.

I'd do some things to win her back,

like beg and weep and crawl.

Move over coffee;

here's's a job for alcohol.

This is a job for alcohol.

It'll show me the way, I'm sure,

Though, I'm not convinced after research,

if it's a poison or a cure.

I've considered other options.

I could be a man, after all.

I could run away, but I'd just die tired;

it's a job for alcohol.

Having a memory is punishment.

There's things best I don't recall.

Move over coffee.

Life's a job for alcohol.

AA BB CC DD

Life is painless for the brainless,
disarming for the charming,
perilous for the hairless,
unengaging for the aging.

Not snuggly for the ugly,
not generic for the cleric,
not spacious for the racist,
still flawless for the bra-less.

Life's lucky for the plucky,
funky for the chunky,
confusing for the losing,
with bad timing for this rhyming.

Cosmic Karma

Think of all the terror T-Rex caused,
with its huge, clawed feet and massive jaws.
Think of all the dino prayers for justice done
sent to dino heaven when it ate a dino son.

T-Rex was never sweet or even saccharine,
so some bad T-Rex karma built up then.
As to those dino prayers, dino gods listened,
and now T-Rex's nearest kin is the chicken.

Here Today, Gone to Mars

It is here and now. It is now and then.
I am up and down, then right back again.
My feet are on Earth, my head's in the stars.
I'm here today, but I'm gone to Mars.

I can be convinced. I can change my mind.
I'll let you decide; I'm the decisive kind.
My mind is closed; it is still ajar.
I'm here today, but I'm gone to Mars.

I'm where I should be, but my mind tends to
stray.
My head's in the game, my heart's far away.
My feet are on Earth, my head's in the stars.
I'm here today, but I'm gone to Mars.

We can walk from here. We can take a bus.
We can walk in pairs, just the three of us.
It's really near. It's really quite far,
if you are here today, then gone to Mars.

It's so quiet here, if you don't mind the sound.
I'm scared we're lost; hope we're never found.
Such a pretty face; lots of ugly scars.
We're all here today, but gone to Mars.

Canada

If you travel a lot, don't be a fool.

Be careful where you go, of course,

'cause the closer you get to Canada,

the more things will eat your horse.

Between Redneck and the Blues

It was easy for my daddy; he was country
through and through,

and it was easy for my mama, she was raised on
Delta blues,

but I grew up in the middle, and I never could
quite choose.

Guess that makes me rockabilly, between
redneck and the blues.

My sister plays the banjo, my brother slide
trombone.

My uncle plays the fiddle, my aunt plays
saxophone.

I hide out in the middle; I don't want to have to
choose

between relatives and relations, between
redneck and the blues.

Chorus:

> Let me live with Wanda Jackson,
>
> Zeb Turner, Billy Monroe.
>
> Not in Nashville or on Bourbon Street
>
> with people I don't know.
>
> Give me honky-tonk and boogie
>
> with Carl Perkins' Blue Suede Shoes.
>
> Let me stay here in the middle,
>
> between redneck and the blues.

> Sometimes they all start fighting. I got cousins
> on both sides.
>
> In between, I keep my head down to keep from
> getting crucified.
>
> There's a lot of music in the family, lots of
> tapping of our shoes;
>
> just don't get beat or bruised or busted between
> redneck and the blues.

Feelings

> How I feel from day to day
>
> really just depends
>
> on where old age has started
>
> and feeling crappy ends.

Philosophy/World View

Getting Comfortable

It may be that this is the last of all time,
in which case it doesn't matter,
or that this goes on for all time,
in which case, it doesn't matter.

But it may be that this is the only time,
and we must make it matter,
because all that matters is time,
and we can't hold time with matter.

Will Color Still Bloom?

When you wake from the dream of living
to describe the foundations you laid,
will your song be of ashes or healing,
temples or escapade?

Will you search for your name on the
parchment?
Will you read of your deeds on the scroll?
Will you cherish the wisdom you garnered?
Will you mourn for the loss of your soul?

Will the world bear new paths where your feet trod?

Will color still bloom where your hands were?

Will the time that you lived mark the living?

Consider. There's still time to answer.

Looking for What I Find

Put to music by Bill Coleman.

Cup of coffee, cigarette,

almost ready, not quite yet.

Long road ahead, same behind,

lots to look for, lots to find.

Juke box playing, pretty good song,

little bit longer, can't stay long.

Just half a cup, one more smoke,

won't make me richer, still not broke.

Chorus:

Cup of coffee, cigarette,

almost ready, not quite yet.

Didn't grow up thinking this was mine,

but I'll keep on looking for what I find.

Friendly waitress, kind of rare.
Ought to tell her I like her hair.
Hope she's a wife, maybe a mother,
hope someone, somewhere, is thinking of her.

Murmured voices, hearty laugh,
price of cattle, price of gas,
could use some rain, grass is brown.
Ship comes in, gonna leave this town.

Screen door opens, tinkling bell;
overalls, work boots, earthy smell.
Clouds are parting, sun might shine.
What I look for is what I find.

You Can't Get It All in One Place

The young have the health, the old have the wealth.

You can't get it all in one place.

In the country it's pretty but the job's in the city.

You can't get it all in one place.

Try as you might, fight the good fight,

You can't get it all in one place.

The love of your life just may not be your wife.

You can't get it all in one place.

Chorus:

There's so much in life worth living.

There's so much we all want to own.

There's so much in life worth saving,

but it's scattered to hell and all gone.

We gather the pieces and try to put more

in our very own personal space,

but what we want most won't fit through the door

'cause you can't get it all in one place.

My very best friend took a job in Berlin.

I can't get it all in one place.

My dream career pays just pennies a year.

I can't get it all in one place.

The car of this dreamer's a spanking new
Beamer,

but I can't get it all in one place.

The car I afford is a nine-year-old Ford.

I can't get it all in one place.

The magazine ads promise steel butts and abs,

but I can't get it all in one place.

The idea's appealing, but the body's not willing.

I can't get it all in one place.

Life has its pains, life has its gains,

and at last it all fits in one place.

Heaven's the goal, but we end up in hole,

where at last it all fits in one place.

The Ticking of a Clock

So much to do, so little time—
important things—like making rhymes,
planning the future, re-arranging the past,
trying to make every minute last.

Awake at dawn, outa bed by noon.
Money in the mail can't arrive too soon.
Car won't start but where would I go?
I am where I am; I know what I know.

Trying to make every minute last.
Just yesterday, hope seemed so vast.
Life lifted me up then tore me down,
now the ticking of a clock is a terrible sound.

A dog chasing his tail thinks he's going real
fast.
Watching dreams die is a way to get past
running out of hope—no dream of mine—
but now that I have it, I feel just fine.

Lonesome Road

Been going down this lonesome road so long,
sometimes I think it's the only one. . .
but lonesome roads are always there.
Crowd's got 'em.
Home's got 'em.

Sometimes on the safest path,
singing high along the way,
no rocks, no holes,
long, flat distances,
single same samenesses,
no bumps,
some soul singing some song sets,
me thinking of other roads,
sings me curves,
sings me hills,
whistles me windey downs into the valleys,
makes the lonesome road so. . .
lonesome.
But some crowds at some intersections
suck up such souls, zoom on,
leave me watching,
kicking stones 'til the dust cloud's gone.

Road climbs after that,
steep, mean climb,
and one look back can topple me off

Colors and Shades

Black people talk Black Language.

Whites speak White when they speak.

In between are shades of in between,

talking and speaking unique.

All the years and culture and training

that generations of men have incurred

are funneled and filtered and finally formed

into all of our daily words.

And each generation of colors and shades

starts afresh to learn what to say.

God give them the wisdom to communicate
clearly,

for they all must learn to speak gray.

The Moments Lost

It seems that there has always been
just one more hurdle, fence to mend,
one more job, move to make,
one more payment, trip to take,
a debt to pay, promise to keep,
more hours of work than hours of sleep,
and yet I know the finest life
is in children's fingers, eyes of a wife,
plans we'd make if we had the chance,
familiar songs, rekindled romance.

But the things we do to continue on,
continue until what we'd keep is gone,
and when we're done, with time to rest,
we've long since passed the briefest best,
and even then there's one task more,
another passage, the final door,
beyond which, perhaps, for all the cost
we'll be paid back for the moments lost.

Neurosis

Is it wisdom that the morning brings
when it tortures what the night did sing,
or is it merely recompense
for all the words I've uttered since
yesterday, when I was so wise
and so unwilling to compromise?
No, 'tis just the old self-doubt
which watches me and seeks me out
each time I chase my lofty dreams,
which some regard as menacing schemes.
'Tis just my mind with dagger drawn,
ambushing hope at crack of dawn,
telling me that love won't last.
Patience, mind, this too shall pass.

Dimensions

If a germ or a virus can live a full life

unaware we exist, for we are so great,

while an ant knows our feet deliver death,

but doesn't attempt to communicate,

and if you can imagine the vastness of space

but can only explore it in movies and books,

then how many dimensions are there left to
find?

How many more have we overlooked?

What drama and pathos are curled in the
cracks

between the tiles of our kitchen floors?

What seasons change and whose harvests
freeze,

when we open and close our closet doors?

What gateways through time, what portals
through space

do our needles create sewing buttonholes?

Is the sand in my pocket a tine galaxy,

or the bones of a lost race's souls?

On Mendacity

The great vague sadistic joke

rattles about but fails to dodge

the minds that grab,

the blinding smoke,

the banter and the persiflage.

I'm holding together the jigsaw clues

and dropping hints in selected places,

but rumors and lies

are yesterday's news

before the truth has tied its laces.

Ideas

Philosophers unite them as useful sarcasms.

Poets apply them as the mind's cataplasms.

Ministers distribute them in iconoclasms.

Ideas, not rules, spark enthusiasms.

Upon the Creation of Artificial Life

I believe in the Great Mystery,

as well as chemistry and time.

I believe in the power of music,

and the inadequacy of rhyme.

I believe there's something out there

but most people have it wrong.

Our time of knowing not is brief;

the time of knowing eternally long.

Living, in Ten

With reason and choice we fashion our fate,

adopt what we need, compose and create,

design what we can, sometimes emulate,

and throughout our youth our minds cultivate.

Then each with our pasts and powers innate,

relying on strength or some opiate,

become proficient or live profligate,

embrace what we love, espouse what we hate,

and goodness invoke, or harm imprecate,

Such is existence, the marvelous fete.

Blues 07/21

This past July did not blow me away;
just blew me along instead,
but it blew in the blues, now just a blur—
t'was a blues blur that blew, 'nuff said.

Blues today with red chili sauce,
blue corn chips with blues tamale.
31 days of home-cooked blues—
life is food, fools, and folly.

Blues, this oh seven two one—
it's a date just like any other—
been 31 days of home-cooked blues
and August just may see another.

Blues so drab they camouflage black,
blues charred a deep sooty brown;
that's what I've got and have had for a month—
blues this oh seven two one.

Found It Where I Left It

Funny that I missed it,
busy planning, I suppose.
Young man won't see what's plain to see,
only what he thinks he knows.

Lots of paths lead to the temple,
if temples are your goal,
but sometimes staying where you are
is the best place for your soul.

Had it, lost it, walked away;
spent years searching again,
then found it where I left it,
right where it's always been.

It's okay to listen to good advice,
then decide what's truly good.
Lots of folks willing to live your life,
or tell you how you should.

Me I listened to my inner voice;
which spoke in some foreign tongue,
and I followed it when I should have stayed
right where it first begun.

Religion

Braille Dots for God

What are the names of the newest angels?
What little names did their mothers say
over and over? "Lord shield him from danger,
deliver her safely, Amen," hear them pray.

The names are scratched on the great rock of
time,
braille dots for God, come Judgement Day,
pockmarks in granite, not sculpture sublime,
on the vast Book of Heaven, the Milky Way.

Edenish Dreams

(Recorded by Bill Coleman as "The Hole in God's Pocket)

We are the lint that fell on the path,

when the Lord decided to walk it,

and blew in the wind He summoned to blow.

We are the hole in God's pocket.

We are the sand that sifts 'neath Heaven's door,

since the Lord decided to lock it,

and litters the floor 'til He sweeps it away.

We are the hole in God's pocket.

We are the grit that grinds in the gears,

and fouls the cogs and the sprockets

of the engine the Lord has scheduled to tune.

We are the hole in God's pocket.

And we are the curl of gray-ish white hair,

tucked inside of a locket,

he wears to remember His Edenish dreams,

before man was the hole in His pocket.

Days Fly By

The days fly by.
The years crawl slowly.
I'm certain I will die;
less certain of what's holy.

Complete Evolution

Folks talk about evolution,
but don't question all its ways;
like does Earth's overpopulation,
means more of us need to turn gay?
A place that improves until the end
is where most folks want to be.
Is that the perfection most religions contend?
Sounds like Heaven to me.

If we each of us do something
to improve the world a bit,
and we keep on making it better,
and don't stop doing it,
then at the end of eternity's road
there's a logical expectation
that evolution's ultimate goal
must be Paradise and perfection.

God's Big Enough

I can't buy my way into Heaven,
Whether I'm rich or poor.
Whichever I be,
I must still find the key,
though admission is free at the door.

I can't talk my way into Heaven.
I should just as well save my breath,
and just thinking it through
won't get me through,
or geniuses would always cheat death.

Chorus:

Some say there's one path to the temple.
Some say there's a million or two.
Some claim they must kill
to do their god's will.
Only God knows why that would be true.
Some say we must learn written gospel.
Some say their hearts hear God's call,
but the burden is man's,
we must all understand.
God's big enough to handle it all.

Some say God's judgment is coming.

Others gladly will judge you for free.

Some claim their behavior

is like that of a savior.

Some admit life's a big mystery.

All I know is that I must keep trying

to do right as I know it to be.

Then when my struggles cease,

perhaps I'll find peace,

and see what God really wants us to see.

Love

Sometimes Sadly

The dust of years was on the shelves
of the closet where we'd stored ourselves
in letters, boxes, and outgrown toys,
the relics of a thousand joys.
The scrap of paper, lined with age,
a single, yellow legal page,
caught my eye and caught my heart;
the forgotten words of you, sweetheart.

I read and smiled to touch again
the strength and hopeful discipline
which guided pen to structured verse
in which you caught our universe,
the times we shared in halting art,
by which to me you did impart,
sometimes sadly, but with truth
the love we knew in shining youth.

I folded it along the crease
Where first you did that night in peace
when the ink was fresh, as was our love,
and I was all you'd written of.
I know that you could not stop time
except with simple, sincere rhyme
which pictured us, as it does yet,
without remorse, without regret.

Before All Our Laces Came Untied

Put to music by Bill Coleman

> I can hide the things that I can't erase,
> but memories leak and run down my face.
> It's a face I refuse to wear in a crowd.
> Everyone has a chapter they don't read aloud.
>
> I want to go back to when it wasn't too late,
> when the way was clear, and the path was
> straight.
> We may have lied to ourselves; not to the
> hearts inside.
> It was before all our laces came untied.

Chorus:

> Before all our laces came untied
> we were never cautious or eagle-eyed.
> We thought having no fate would be our fate.
> Now I want to go back to when it wasn't too
> late.
>
> I know you loved me. Guess you let it pass.
> You didn't know my heart was made of glass.
> Now it's cracked and covered in a smoky cloud;
> part of the chapter I will not read aloud.

Donita

Put to music by Bill Coleman

Donita, you were always there

to comfort me and stroke my hair,

to listen to things I had to say.

When my world was out of kelter

you were there to give me shelter.

Donita please don't ever go away.

Since I was five you've been with me.

You've followed me so faithfully;

a love like yours is mighty hard to find,

But in spite of all you do,

there is one thing wrong with you—

Donita, you live only in my mind.

Chorus:

Donita you live only in my mind, in my mind.

You're the dream girl that I've always hoped to find.

No other girl has been so true;

they do me wrong, I come home to you.

Donita, you live only in my mind.

Donita was my first true love,
the only girl I could think of,
but she was six and I was only five.
When I was ten she moved away
and I haven't seen her to this day,
but in my mind I've kept her love alive.

Perhaps some day some sweet young thing
will take your place and wear my ring
and be the girl that I will make my wife,
but 'til that day please stay with me;
you know my needs so perfectly.
Donita, you're the dream girl of my life.

Another Dream Girl

A shy little girl, 20 years ago,

stole my heart, plenty years ago,

but I let her keep it, 20 years or so;

thought she'd need it, plenty years to go.

Then I called her up just the other day,

just to stay in touch, just to hear her say

"Who?"

L'amour et la Fumee ne Peuvent se Cacher

(Love and smoke cannot be hidden)

Must I my heart deny

and brandish on my sleeve

some stoic alibi

and thereby find reprieve

for my thoughts and actions shameless,

for the joy I've always sought,

in the hope that I'm held blameless

in someone else's thoughts?

The rhetoric I speak of

'tis theory, nothing more,

for I've trumpeted my love

ab imo la pectore (from the heart's depths)

49

The Avoidance of Portia

(Portia is a female character and protagonist in Shakespeare's "The Merchant of Venice").

A passion, delicate, which did not shrink

from union with its unpledged object

was experienced wise, or so it seemed,

in the mind of its dark-haired subject.

But passion, stirred, is the mind's slave not,

tho' sure to bend to its urging.

'Tis the heart's bondsman, and will be fecund

through only those masteries merging.

Time cares not, but apportions our cares

with no regard for our scheming.

Let not its flight find regret, ill-bred,

for today, my Portia, dreaming.

Without You

Without you birds still sing and fly.

Without you the sea still hugs the shore.

Without you the sky is still the sky.

I'm not surprised by that anymore.

You left and the world keeps turning.

I'll never forgive it for that.

You left and the sun keeps burning.

The sun's not a diplomat.

Honeymoon Song

To the melody of "Abraham's Daughter."

Patricia this is quite a time;

this time that I have known you,

but Lord, I do believe it is

the time that I was born to.

Together we will learn so much

of life and of each other,

for now that I have found you dear

there'll never be another.

My life with you will see law books
and sweat-stained English saddles,
plus tales of people now long gone
and their forgotten battles.

I plan to spend my life with you
'mid our horses and our heroes,
for God knows you are right for me.
I do believe that He knows.

So take my hand Patricia, love,
let's see what life has for us.
Time's melody is playing now
its sweetest, longest chorus.

Fragments of Symmetry

I toured an old residence, much too hastily,

and gaped at the glimpses of your history.

I found porcelain, flawless, not relic remains,

crumbs for my feasting, ephemeral grains.

I confessed with abandon, acts which have
jaded.

You hinted, in passing, of flowers unfaded,

vice not experienced, fresh virtue unshaken.

I've given too often; from you, it was taken.

We may continue, as portions, through
occupation,

but time is too fleet to not extend invitation.

Come sing your completion, the song's writing
is mine.

We might, by our music, these loose fragments
entwine.

What Did She Do?

When did I first become suspicious?

What gave me the very first clue?

How did I learn not to trust her?

What exactly did she do?

It wasn't so in the beginning,

for then I loved her so.

Back then I'd die before turning away,

or ever letting her go.

But now I know my error,

and hate the fool I've been.

I hope I die long years before

I love such as her again

I Could Never Love You More

Once we had a world together.
Now that bird has flown.
It's a shame we laughed together,
but now must cry alone.

If we could do it all again,
if we had youth restored,
I'd try to love you better.
I could never love you more.

Chorus: Without you the sky is still the sky.
  I'm not surprised by that anymore.
  I wish I'd loved you better,
  but I could never have loved you more.

I've left my door wide open,
though you'll never knock again.
My world depends on fantasy
and things that have never been.

In my mind I reject the apologies
I know will never come.
My mind creates anthologies
to explain what we've become.

She Was a Keeper

She was a keeper who'd never been kept.

He was a weeper who had never wept.

All of their stories were of being alone.

The little they knew was mostly unknown.

To see his skin without the scars

was like seeing sky without the stars.

None of his wounds speared to the bone,

but some still bleed when she cries alone.

Chorus: She was a keeper who had never been
kept.

He was a weeper who had never wept,

but when she left, unkept, still a prize,

the hint of a tear was in one of his eyes.

He said, "I love you." She said, "It'll pass."

Perhaps it will or it already has.

Traces of love can become angry scars

that fill the sky of a soul with angry stars.

Death

Chuckie Death

Charles Falhaber was a close friend and fraternity brother who was killed in an automobile accident in 1973.

Chuckie and I drove yellow spinning wheel
buses
in soft drumming rain,
in early morning yawns and shivers,
in university days and fraternity nights, in
1972.

Black hair exploded from beneath ballon jean
hat,
flew in the wind of our chariots,
with blue eyes and crop-bearded grins,
pirate chic, not clown fashion, in 1972.

One night as I studied the law of the land
Chuckie bowed knightly and kissed Mary's
hand,
drove away from her love into deep Dallas
night,
was alone in the street at 2 a.m. red light,
when out of the sky, like a black falling star,
hurled a drunk in a Buick onto Chuckie's still
car.

Another lane, another street, another two
minutes,
either way, any direction, and the news
would have tsked tsked about control,
concrete medians, going up drunk,
coming down, clunk; not Chuckie death.

But time and place and idle choices
came together on Lovers Lane,
and though the years will deal more death
cards
and have more in the pack,
none will be Chuckie death,
for he was my first closest,
whom I'll remember the longest.

One Moment

November rustles her feathers,

plucks the downy leaves that strew our path.

Beyond the hills where we walk,

the sky is freezing blue, gradually—

a noticeable sort of afternoon.

We honor the changing seasons

and turn toward home when a solitary figure,

distant, familiar, stops to gaze our direction

for one moment, long enough to reach, then he
is gone

quite before we knew, lost in the noticeable
afternoon,

now strangely cold.

Before I Catch on Fire

Please hit me with a tie rod
before you throw me on the pyre.
I'd like to be unconscious
before I catch on fire.

Please make sure my rubber collar
is not steel-belted tire.
I'd just as soon not suffocate
before I catch on fire.

Be sure to string my meat hook
with acoustic piano wire,
so I can end it on a high note
before I catch on fire.

Falling Leaves

You touch it for an instant then move on,
twenty years here, sixty years there.
You've just arrived and then you're gone,
no notion when, many theories where.

That's how it is, but do not grieve.
Make some moments resonate.
Trees don't live for fallen leaves,
nor folks here for those now late.

Epilogue

When I'm dead and in the ground
you may sometimes wish me still around.
Something will happen that makes you smile,
reminds you of me for a little while,
and you'll wonder what I'd say if there,
but you can't know and shouldn't care.

Know while alive I thought a bit,
though not always clearly, I'll admit,
but I found it helped, or was no worse
if I captured thoughts in structured verse,
and over the years I collected those lines,
which may be all I will leave behind.

Oh Burning Youth

To the tune of "Skibbereen" and included in Bill and Carla Coleman's CD "The Haunting War" in 2005.

Oh burning youth, how hot it blazed,
how promising its flame.
It promised me much more than this;
I thought it promised fame,
but now that youth has burned away,
I have no joys but one,
and he now burns with youthful fire.
Don't go to war my son.

Dear son, my only son,
the treasure of my life,
Someday you'll know what I have learned
and understand my strife.
You'll find that men in highest power—
it's always been this way—
they take you from your father's home
for reasons they'll not say.

They promise things they have no right
to promise to the young.

They'll preach the patriotic words,
promise stars and moon and sun;
but with your lives they find a way
to line their purse with gold,
and leave your aged father
lone with no more joy to hold.

Oh, let me now protect you son
as ever I have done.
Put away the sharpened bayonet;
please put away the gun.
A hiding place I'll make for you
where safe you'll always be,
so you may grow old and have a son
and someday feel as me.

My son, my son, he did not hear
or did not choose to feel.
He marched away with other sons
into the battlefields.
And now he lies in some far grave,
unmarked, forever gone,
and all I have are memories
and the message of this song.

Too Much

They may say it was too much alcohol,

or all that nicotine.

They may agree I drove too fast

or used too much sugar and cream.

Whatever it is, it will have been too much,

they'll agree as they dry their tears,

for it's always too much when it's finally too
much,

even if it's just the years.

Family/Friends

Our Father's Art

On the occasion of a special show of the Akers family crafts at the Lipscomb County, Texas Museum.

Among these paintings, these quilts, these
poems,

these crafts, these songs, these books,

among this family's efforts and treasures,

these contributions we look . . .

. . . but where is Edward's art?

Is your father not creative?

"Our father creative? Oh no. 'Twas our mother.

See her works there?

We inherited all we do from her,

while father is no more artist than styler of
hair."

Unless, perhaps, on some Herford's hip

a particularly legible bar-nine brand,

or on a corral with baling wire,

some useful repair by his hand

Unless, perhaps, . . . there is other art,

such as braving the Great Depression

without a father of his own

to fall back on when challenges grew.

Just he, and her, together, alone,

enduring drought, hail, tornado,

rising back up each time slapped down

by Nature, life, needs, pain,

when cattle died or crops turned brown,

and he with only labor, sweat, grit,

his word as collateral to the bank,

and never to foreclosure sank.

Unless, perhaps . . .

it is being the neighbor to whom all could turn

for aid, no matter when, or what the task;

being regarded as absolutely dependable,

reliable, whom a man need only ask

for help, whether farmer, preacher, or lonely
drunk,

the latter, who sometimes after midnight yelled

for Edward to come out and talk, who would,

for he also the claim of neighbor held.

Unless, perhaps . . .
it is being pillar to community, church,
schools, serving calmly, steady,
without boast, pride, greed, self-gain;
only being when called, ready
to perform the service needed
for nearly eighty years
and regretting only, when older,
the calls no longer appeared.

Or unless, perhaps . . .
it is a marriage of sixty-five years,
four children who each left the nest
but could always turn back
for support, help, advice, and best,
gave him children and their children
who could say they knew him, will recall
him as real, not monument or legend,
though he will always be to all.

No, our father is not creative.
No art is his, here, on display,
except perhaps our everything,
and all we are today.

David Lived Life

David lived life like there would be no
tomorrow,

huge in his joy, huge in his sorrow,

reached up in the sky to invisible shelves,

raked down new ways to look at ourselves.

David loved life and he loved life truly.

Everything that was him was loud and unruly.

Great booming voice, great roaring laughter,

words down to the ground, thoughts up to the
rafters.

I've never known a man like David McCartney.

He was ten parts everyone and one part me.

Then an afternoon nap brought an end to his
tomorrow,

left us huge in our loss and huge in our sorrow.

David and Kelly

A white-haired man and his blue-eyed wife,
big in my mind, bigger than life,
could fill a house with the power of thought,
could pour delight from a coffee pot,
roared laughter at life from a windbound hill,
are living there now, are laughing there still.

If life was the prize instead of the race,
we'd each have our all in a single place,
wouldn't leave behind what we'd take along,
would draw dearest ones with a piper's song,
and I'd be on that hill, roaring at life,
with that white-haired man and his blue-eyed
wife.

To Patty, Nathan, and Megan

How novel that poetry, the art

which so often bares the innermost heart,

should be so sparse in these happiest times,

while past misery inspired so many rhymes.

How odd that now that I've found my all,

the love, the son, the daughter, that doll,

the ideal mate, each an image of me,

that I should neglect my poetry.

Instead, I should yell and shout and sing,

and tell the reader, if any, each thing

that makes life perfect, how now it's mine,

and explain how it's more than "special" or
"fine."

I've survived all the maudlin, mawkish mess

that sparked love poems and cries of distress.

I've found a Nirvana—life as it should be,

and the least it deserves is some poetry.

Politics And The Nation

Do Not Make Me President

Do not make me president,

for I will squander every cent

the corporations have stockpiled

on loathsome poor and wretched child.

I'll surrender all our strength

and go to almost any length

to cause the needed wars to cease

in favor of unneeded peace.

Advice from wise men I'll avoid.

I'll call our generals paranoid.

No more missiles will I build.

To pleas for friendship I will yield.

To foreign threats I will be blind,

and just to prove I've lost my mind,

to world affairs, the Golden Rule,

I will apply, I'm such a fool.

No, don't put me in your lead.

A greater mind is what you need—

one not confused by wild thoughts of

faith and hope and Christian love.

NYC

I'm a visitor in NYC,

where everything is pricey.

Bought an autographed photo of Christ,

but I'm sure it was overpriced.

Women I Saw Naked

I got to count 'em, 'cause if not,

or if there's one that I forgot,

or three or four not even there—

some fantasies or in underwear—

then folks might think I'm negligent,

and out of the race for president.

A fella's got to wash his clothes,

never ever pick his nose,

zip his pants, clip his nails,

stay outa bars and outa jails,

and never ever be flatulent,

if he plans on being president.

And being caught at having lied
is nickel-plated suicide.
It's like your lie's the very worst,
and can't possibly be the very first,
because no one the least fraudulent
can dream of becoming president.

So I've decided the important things—
got a count on my offspring,
ran the tests for the odd disease,
dipped my cat and dog for fleas,
and next it's women I can document
I saw naked before I was president.

Can't be like them that weren't prepared
for questions that got them all ensnared,
and the papers make it sound routine
that the number of women a fella's seen
naked is somehow pertinent
to holdin' the office of president.

So let's see, my mom's the first,
then my sister, then that nurse . . .
then that girl in Omaha . . . .

Some Views of the Country

Some views from our windshields were the
same from their coaches;

the white-columned mansions, the tree-lined
approaches,

some meadows, some woodlands, some bowers
and arbors,

the surging slow rivers, the ocean calm
harbors,

and deep in this Earth roots are anchored and
set

of our future—the past we must never forget.

This land has seen stirring, struggle, and
striving,

awakening, accepting, America arriving.

Here endurance was tested and emotions were
torn,

sweet hopes were blasted but new hopes were
born.

Now the nation goes forward, anxious to move

toward progress and greatness, so much to
improve.

Where once there was splendor, now ruins
often lie.

Where stood virgin timber, now cities stretch
high.

In these places the struggles have long ago
ceased,

but the force of those struggles are the source
of our peace.

We'll not know completeness if in frenzied
pursuits

we forget where we came; we abandon our
roots.

Trump

This world has so many haters,

who don't see what he represents.

Don't those pundits and commentators

believe we need him to be president?

Perhaps he's dishonest and racist,

but I am here to announce:

he's just an adjudicated rapist,

and a felon on 34 counts.

American Highways

Drive through guns and discount liquor,

used car lots, Jesus bumper sticker.

Farmers' market, corn and cucumbers.

"How's my driving?" Dial a toll-free number.

Round bales for sale, exit next right;

speed limit's 60, 55 at night.

IHOP, Golden Arches, Dairy Queen ahead,

barbecue and steaks, Angus grain-fed.

Chorus:

Driving these American highways,

looking at tomorrow's by-gone days,

wondering what will be when this is gone.

Can't see it or stop it; best move on.

Cell towers in a field, guy wires and anchors,

over-sized loads, silver gas tankers,

calves, lambs, and foals—petting zoo cute;

12 acres for sale, will build to suit.

Hate

Communists, Nazis, Ku Klux Klan,

Proud Boys, Oath Keepers, Taliban,

terrorists, atheists, racists too—

hate keeps them going. What's it do for you?

Protestants, protesters, PETA, the Pope,

wet backs, MAGA hats, horoscopes,

tree huggers, gun nuts, illegals, ex-wives—

each has its haters; somehow each survives.

Confederates, Conservatives, commercials on
TV,

Liberals, Mormons, I think you'll all agree,

there's always someone, somewhere, easy to
despise.

Love will make some people low; but hate can
get some high.

THE GREAT ORANGE MYSTERY

(to the tune of Battle Hymn of the Republic)

> We have heard the insane ramblings of the man named Donald Trump
>
> We have witnessed MAGA crazies fawn and kiss his massive rump.
>
> We can't believe that voters will still listen to that chump,
>
> but Trump goes blundering on.
>
> Why so many love him is the great orange mystery.
>
> He won although more people cast their votes for Hillary.
>
> No candidate has been as inept in U.S. history,
>
> and Trump goes lumbering on.

Chorus:

> It's not the party of Lincoln
>
> It's not the party of Lincoln
>
> It's not the party of Lincoln
>
> It's the party of lost souls.

What used to be the GOP is now a gang of
clowns,

since they chose a pumpkin and handed him
the crown.

It started several years ago, and then it melted
down

as Trump came marching on.

In a contest in the GOP to find the biggest
clown,

Matt, Marjorie, or Lauren might have won
hands down,

but the party found a pumpkin and handed
him the crown,

and Trump goes bungling on.

The lies he tells amaze us but each day he tells
some more.

It's time our nation's voters show this fool the
door.

This election's become personal and not unlike
a war,

and Trump goes stumbling on.

He caused an insurrection; it was very plain to
see,

and 34 convictions should make everyone
agree,

a felon and a rapist should not be the nominee,
but Trump goes waddling on.

He's insulted everyone from Milwaukee to
McCain.
He calls our veterans losers, holds our heroes
in disdain.
Why anyone can't see the truth is totally
insane,
but Trump goes spluttering on.

He said the J-6 radicals were heroes treated
wrong,
when they were sent to prison where they all
belong.
There's no end to stupid things claimed by
Diaper Don.
His lies go marching on.

He loves himself and no one else, but doesn't
realize
normal people do not see what he sees through
his eyes.
Yet his supporters keep on listening to all his
crazy lies,
and Trump goes blustering on.

Storytelling

The Old Soldier

Written in 1966 at age 16. Put to music by Bill Coleman for his CD "The Haunting War" (2005).

The old man sat in the general store
in his usual place, the chair by the door.
He loosened the straps on his wooden leg,
and frowned as he leaned it against a keg,
for this was his token of the glories of war;
his own Medal of Honor he'd nearly died for.

The child who had clung to his mother's hand
slowly approached the grizzled old man.
As he stared at the stump in disbelief,
he tried to imagine what kind of thief
would steal a man's leg and leave one of wood
that didn't look like a man's leg should.

It puzzled the boy and he wanted to ask
"Where's your real leg?" but it'd be quite a task,
for the old man looked fierce, with his stubby
gray beard
and ragged old suit that made him look rather
weird,
but the old eyes were soft, so the lad finally
dared,
and the old man's frown faded as memory
flared.

His mind raced back to another time,
and he heard the guns roar and heard the shells
whine.
He heard the drums beat and he saw the men
die,
and he heard that last shell come out of the sky.
He felt the shell his, as it did years ago,
and he heard the doc say, "Your leg's got to go."

He remembered the pain as the knife cut his
skin
and then as the bone saw ground through his
limb.
He remembered his screams, but men held him
down
until it was over. He was laid on the ground.
He remembered the weeks when nothing was
clean
and the smell of his flesh as it rot from
gangrene.

He remembered the months he lay flat on his
back
with a stump for a leg, swollen and black;
then finally crutches, then wood for a leg,
and the years he survived by learning to beg,
until now an old man who just sat by the door
and lived off the scraps that were left for the
poor.

How do you make a small child understand
That the hell that is war is designed by man;
That the world can be in such a sad state
That all some men know is the best way to
hate?
So he looked at the child, and said with a
cough,
"It was a long time ago. A bear bit it off."

One Man's Dream

A boy had a dream, and he became a man

who nursed that dream, and it became a plan

that he set in motion over many years

while he married, had children and built a
career.

But he clung to the dream despite loss and
delays,

knew he would do so to the end of his days.

Then at last it happened, just before he retired.

The plan came together, grew wings, got wired!

So he rushed to his wife to share the news so
dear

but she was watching TV, didn't care, didn't
hear.

Oh well.

The Good Marriage

He followed Patton into Germany.

She waited for him back in Tennessee.

She gave him a daughter and two fine sons.

He found good work; never failed them once.

There was no regret in the tone of his voice,

when Vietnam took one of his boys.

They lived the American dream quite well,

in a time and place unparalleled.

But the years took more than youth and good
looks.

It closed her sweet mind like a man shuts a
book.

Now she sits alone at a slot machine.

He sits close by, should she call for him.

She knows how to play, what buttons to choose,

doesn't care if she wins, doesn't mind to lose,

doesn't know where she is, even who she is,

but what's his is hers and what's hers is his.

Big Sweet Kid

A big, sweet kid with Down's Syndrome
used to ride the school bus on his way home.
Didn't ride it in the mornings, was in a special
program;
answered every question with "Yessir/No
Mam."

Most of the kids would just ignore him,
but a backseat boy had a hardon for him,
used to shoot spit wads, called him Feeb and
Ding Dong,
would shout "yassah/no mam" in falsetto sing
song.

But the big, sweet kid didn't understand,
would turn in his seat, smile, wave his hand,
look the boy in the eye, let his sweet look linger,
and the boy in the back seat would give him the
finger.

Then one day the bus had a front tire blowout.
It was wintertime, there was ice and snow out.
The kids hooted and cursed, filled the air with
satire.
We got out on the street, stood staring at the
flat tire.

The driver found the jack, two big boys got the
spare.

Driver loosened all the lugs, jacked the bus into
the air,

had the flat tire off, but when he turned his
back

to pick up the spare, the bus slipped off the
jack.

Another place, another time, another outcome
all so nice,

perhaps some summer day, without that patch
of ice

where the hub crashed down, bounced, skidded
on the street,

and came to rest atop the boy from the bus's
back seat.

You may think you know what happened, but
you don't nearly.

I don't know what happened, and I swear I saw
it clearly.

All I'm sure of is the reason this outcome was
not tragic

is because that big, sweet kid was somehow
painted all in magic.

Perhaps it was adrenaline, or an optical
illusion.

Perhaps we were stricken with hysterical
confusion.

We knew that big, sweet kid could not lift a
school bus,

but we later all agreed—our eyes did not fool
us.

The Monday next, the big, sweet kid had a front
seat window

when the backseat boy got on, limped down the
center row.

He paused, looked back, grinned and let it
linger,

and as he limped away, he gave the kid the
finger.

No Surprises

She lived her entire life with no surprises,
parties, love, or sweepstakes prizes.
Never mastered the art of small talk chatter,
couldn't understand why such things matter.

Couldn't recall names after introductions,
never opened the door to sweet seduction.
Spent her entire life in the same small city,
always understood that she wasn't pretty.

Chorus:

And she cried some nights and some occasions,
when she pondered too much about implications
of age and shyness and not being pretty.
Although her heart screamed, "Now!" her head wasn't ready.

Toward the end of her years she became the wife
of an imaginary man, bigger than life,
who filled her home with the power of thought,
and poured delight from a coffee pot.

She married that man in a secret place.
They honeymooned on a star in space,
then moved to a cottage on a windy hill.
They're living there now, laughing there still.

She doesn't cry anymore on any occasions.
Doesn't waste time pondering implications
of being shy and not very pretty.
Her heart screamed "Now!" and her mind
made ready.

If life was the prize instead of the race,
we'd each have our all in a single place;
wouldn't leave behind whom we'd take along;
would draw dearest ones with a piper's song.

A Texas Girl

A Texas girl went to New York City.

It was big and she was pretty.

It was dirty but she was pure.

She didn't change it. It didn't change her.

She came back home to Abilene,

told her friends of the wonders she had seen.

Each smiled and nodded, but thought as she
sat,

that she'd rather be dead than ruined like that.

Sewer Rat and Bohunk

On a winter day on a one-horse farm,

on the Texas plains near Podunk,

a white pussy cat

named Sewer Rat,

met a white puppy dog named Bohunk.

Now pussy cats and puppy dogs

are enemies, the bitterest,

but Sewer Rat

was a diplomat,

and Bohunk was cat-illiterate.

So the furry pair became famous pals

on that one-horse prairie farm,

and at first

the very worst

they did was no cause for alarm.

Oh yes, they hassled a heifer,

and maybe they chased some chicks,

but it was just for fun,

no harm done,

just puppy dog/pussy cat tricks.

Then on a fateful winter morning,
Sewer Rat hatched a scheme.
"I'll bet in Podunk,"
he said to Bohunk,
"there's more fun than we ever dreamed."

"I'll bet there's mice for my catching,
and cars for you to chase.
There's bound to be more
maybe glories galore,
than around this boring old place.

So off they set for the city,
excited to be off on a lark,
and for several miles
they were all chatter and smiles,
'til they noticed the sky turning dark.

Thunder and lightening so frightening,
came with rain in gimongous drops.
With no place to hide,
soaked to the hide,
they soon looked like a couple of mops.

At last the sun came out to dry them,
and soon they were able to grin.
They walked on awhile,
maybe a mile,
but the weather turned ugly again.

The wind blew colder and colder.
The sun disappeared in a cloud.
They kept on going,
but it started snowing.
"I'm freezing!" poor Bohunk bow-wowed.

The snow covered up the prairie,
the road, the dog, and the cat.
In the saddest of moods,
Sewer Rat mewed,
"We're lost! Where can Podunk be at?!"

When the blizzard at last subsided,
and snow stopped filling the skies,
what they saw was more funk,
instead of Podunk.
New trouble greeted their eyes.

Ahead on the road was a coyote. (*pronounced*
"Kai-yote")
Sewer Rat arched his back.
He knew that this stranger
meant serious danger,
'cause to coyotes this pair was a snack.

See, coyotes just love little kittens,
and puppies are wonderful too.
For them nothing's funner,
than maybe roadrunner,
to put in a coyote stew.

"Run, Sewer Rat," whispered Bohunk.
"Get away while I slow him up!"
"No, you go ahead,"
the pussy cat said,
"I'm ready to die for you, Pup!"

The coyote came closer and closer.
Gamely the pair stood their ground.
Then they both stared aghast,
as the beast trotted past,
unaware the white pair was around!

When his heart had slowed to a rumble,
Bohunk declared with a scowl,
"The next time you roam,
please leave me at home.
This trip's been too much for me, pal."

Sewer Rate twitched his whiskers,
and sadly, slowly, said,
"I think you're right,
but it's almost night,
and we've got miles to go on ahead."

They trudged up a hill sad and gloomy,
then stopped and stared 'cross the snow,
for in front of their eyes
lay a joyous surprise—
the farm, their home, lay below.

"Yippee-skip!" barked the bouncing Bohunk.
"Hal-a-loo! mewed Sewer Rat,
"there's only one place
for my kitty face,
and home is right where it's at!"

No more did those pals seek adventure.
No more did they ever roam.
'cause now they both knew,
as I'm sure you do too,
that there's nowhere near nice as home.

History

I Met a Man Who Knew a Man

I met a man who knew a man

who rode with Clark Quantrill,

and another who once shook the hand

of the famous Buffalo Bill.

In Virginia is the widow of a boy

who served under Robert E. Lee,

and in Texas is the daughter of a slave,

from when America wasn't free.

A preacher in northern Montana

was there when a baby was born,

whose proud Ogallala grandpa

counted coup at the Little Horn.

And my grandpa used to go on sprees

with bourbon and devil rum,

and sometimes took along Temple,

Sam Houston's youngest son.

When it's bound in books and taught in schools
or flashed on a movie screen,
our history seems too distant,
and dead as a mausoleum.

But as near as the nearest retirement home
as near as each family tree,
our past is there for the touching,
as alive as you or me.

Little Bighorn Artifacts

Come gaze upon these bits of lead,
and iron and brass and bone.
Yearn to see what they have seen
and learn what they have known.
They've held their tongues for a hundred years
in the coarse Montana sod
while mem have sought to unlock their tale,
known now to none but God.

No plow has touched this Springfield shell
nor concrete hid this broken knife,
since they were dropped by frantic men
who fought in vain for life.
No horse this spur has urged to flight,
no belt this buckle held;
each piece has truly held its ground
since their masters all were felled.

For long dark years, their vigil kept,
not touched nor seen by men,
They've waited those who followed Yates
And rode with Crittendon.
They've awaited those whom last they saw
that 25th of June,
the brothers, Boston, Tom, and George,
and Margaret's James Calhoun.

Awaited Keogh with his dancing eyes

and merry Irish laugh,

awaited Cooke with his long sideburns

who served on the Colonel's staff,

awaited Porter, Sturgis, and Lord,

three who were never found,

and two hundred more who were fated to die

on Little Bighorn's bloody ground.

But now these relics sing to those

who can hear their silent song

of moments brief when myths were born,

of mortals, brave but gone.

Come gaze upon these jewels of yore,

once lost and left behind.

Now found, they touch the American heart

and tease the adventuresome mind.

Eva Braun

Young Eva Braun tumbled to history,

fell in love with an evil mystery,

was loyal and true for the whole damned ride;

proved herself with cyanide.

Civil War

Jackson and Janie

The story of Stonewall Jackson's affection for little Jane Corbin is depicted in the movie "Gods and Generals." The following poem was put to music by Bill and Carla Coleman for their CD "The Last Roses" (2001). I have seen grown men weep when Bill sang it to an audience.

The winter between the victories,

the second of the war,

when Jackson lived behind her house

those months that numbered four,

Janie Corbin, five years old,

of the place called Corbin's Hall,

did what Lincoln's men could not,

and captured Old Stonewall.

No cannonade nor mass assault,

no drum nor marching tune,

were needed for her to win the day

when she visited each afternoon.

Armed with trustful eye, wealth of curl,

unspoiled ways and smile,

her strategy much more than matched

his battlefield genius guile.

Chorus:

> And he thought of his own Julia,
> then a babe at Cottage Home,
> and he must have tried to live for a while
> in a world he would never own,
> for between his Julia and five years old
> was a place called Chancellorsville,
> and a hole in the heart of all the South
> that time would never heal.

> One day as he taught Janie lessons
> of the powers of pen or prayer,
> she listened and gazed into his eyes,
> then brushed away her hair.
> "Where's your comb?" Old Stonewall asked.
> "Broken," was her reply,
> and the old blue light he was famous for
> came sparkling in his eyes.
> He took his fine new forage cap,
> the one with the golden band,
> the one he'd worn at Fredericksburg
> when he'd never looked so grand.
> He'd worn it with the new uniform
> J.E.B. Stuart had endowed,
> and it splendored him so dramatically,
> Lee's entire army was proud.

With a few quick snips with a sharpened blade,
he removed the gilded lace,
picked out the threads and held it up
before sweet Janie's face.
Then binding the gold in her golden hair,
he smiled at her tenderly.
"Those curls will stay in place," he said,
If you'll wear this just for me."

Janie Corbin squealed with child's delight
and with firmest sincerity,
vowed she'd wear it all her days,
which, sadly, came to be,
for scarlet fever on cat's paws crept
before Spring was four weeks old,
and stole from Janie Corbin
her unspoiled five-year soul.

When Stonewall Jackson heard the news,
that his little friend had died,
that mighty Jehovah-warrior,
hanged his head and cried.
Joy doesn't linger in some men's lives.
It's not something they can keep,
and Janie Corbin was the very last
to make Old Stonewall weep.

As for the golden band, like all her things,
it was delivered to cleansing flame,
as was done in those days when the fever
claimed another living name.
And of all the lost treasures of this world,
A southern heart understands,
that very few could shine as bright
as that simple golden band.

After reading that Jane's items were burned for fear of contamination and writing the foregoing, I learned that the golden band still exists in a private collection. A photo of it follows.

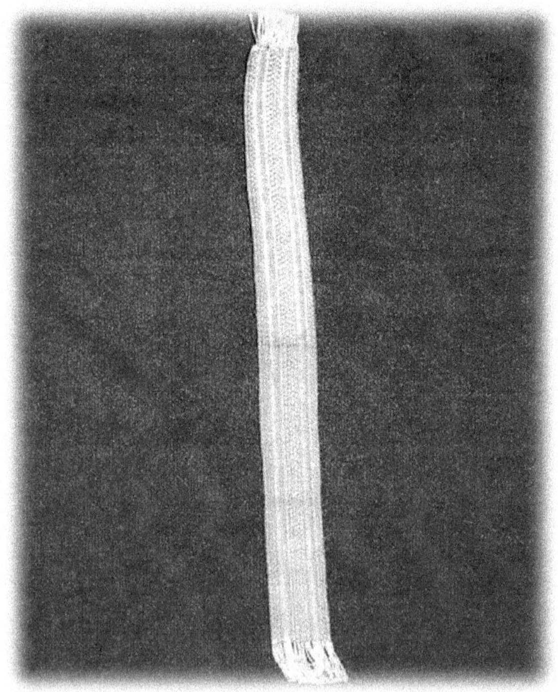

The Southern Birthright

Politically incorrect today but a favorite among many Southerners, Bobby Horton put the lyrics to music and included it in his "Homespun Songs of the C.S.A, Vol. 6" CD in 2001. Others made it the subject of YouTube videos.

> There's a birthright that each southern boy
>
> inherits when he's born,
>
> and he carries it forever,
>
> 'til the day his mourners mourn.
>
> It's not founded in old politics
>
> of race or slavery,
>
> and folks who see no more than that
>
> care not for history.

Chorus:

> For our hearts are still with Jackson
>
> and our faith's in General Lee.
>
> We still can taste the sweetness
>
> of that one last victory.
>
> Though we'll never ride with Stuart,
>
> and we'll never march with Bragg,
>
> we will love our southern heroes
>
> and the old Confederate flag.

It's the way of life that ended,
and the way it died so hard.
It's the honor and the chivalry
folks today most disregard.
It's the Ride Around McClellan
and New Market's young cadets.
It's Sam Watkins telling stories,
and Sam Davis's regret.

Chorus:

For our hearts are still with Jackson
and our faith's in General Lee.
We still can taste the sweetness
of that one last victory.
Though we'll never ride with Stuart,
and we'll never march with Bragg,
we will love our southern heroes
and the old Confederate flag.

It's the dream of Pickett charging,

and never being stopped.

It's the thought of Stonewall Jackson,

never being shot.

Oh, we'd never change America.

She is as she should be,

but we can't help but try to win

just one more victory.

Chorus:

For our hearts are still with Jackson

and our faith's in General Lee.

We still can taste the sweetness

of that one last victory.

Though we'll never ride with Stuart,

and we'll never march with Bragg,

we will love our southern heroes

and the old Confederate flag…

A Hundred Yards From The Wall

Put to music and recorded by Bill Coleman as "The Angel of Marye's Heights" and included in his and Carla's CD "The Last Roses" (2001).

I came to the army as McClellan was leaving,

marched south under Burnside as the air became chilled,

stopped at a river beside an old city,

beneath gentle heights and a wide-open field.

At the top was a wall where Lee's army was waiting,

and rumors ran rampant that Burnside would fight.

I asked an old man what the name of the hill was,

and he said he believed it was called Marye's Heights.

We crossed the pontoons and moved into the city.

At the foot of the heights we unslung our packs.

Writing in pencil on used cartridge papers,

we used nipple picks to pin names to our backs.

I shivered with cold, dread, fear, and loathing.

The upcoming battle would be my first fight.

Perhaps the devil wasn't waiting above me,

but I was certain no angels occupied Marye's
Heights.

We leaned up the hill like a stiff wind was
blowing.

I stared at the ground, tried to pretend I was
calm,

took one step at a time, ignored horror around
me,

held tight to my rifle, prayed the 23rd Psalm.

I didn't see how our lines melted around me,

had no idea I'd be one of the last who would
fall,

and when three bullets found me, I was to
hurled toward the heavens

and dropped in a heap a hundred yards from
the wall.

It wasn't the pain, but the thirst that awoke me.

I was froze to the ground by the blood I had
bled.

I lay in the dark with my mind filled with
terror.

Before half an hour passed, I prayed to be dead.

I guess that I screamed because somebody found me.

He gave me a drink and had kind words to say.

He took off his coat and covered me with it.

When I looked the next morning, that great coat was gray.

On the blood-frozen field above that colonial city,

with no water, no blankets, no fires, and no packs,

thousands of wounded froze to death in the darkness.

They're in marked graves today if they had names on their backs.

The hell we endured was man's, not the devil's,

and I should have died in my very first fight.

I prayed that I would, but a miracle happened—

I was saved by an angel on Marye's Heights.

Jolly Came Riding

Manson Jolly's story is worthy of a movie. These lyrics were put to music by Bill Coleman and included in his and Carla's CD "The Haunting War, (2005).

Five dead Yankees for each brother,

said Manse Jolly in '64,

and if 25 is not enough,

then 25 each or maybe more

killed in bushwhack, South Carolina,

killed in vengeance for what's done,

For two long years Manse Jolly

had damnyankees on the run.

Ain't no number safe together

where Manse Jolly waits alone.

Ain't no use in begging mercy

ain't no way to atone.

He's just one Goddamned rebel

fighting after the war is done.

It's just one long string of vengeance;

won't change a thing of what's been done.

Chorus:

> When Manse Jolly came a-riding
> his mare, Dixie, guns a-blaze.
> It was Hell in South Carolina,
> more hell than a man should raise.
> Manse Jolly took his vengeance
> for five brothers the Yankees killed.
> He took more than a hundred,
> but he never took his fill.

> Manson Jolly might still be there,
> killing Yankees to this day,
> but they said they'd take his family
> and put them far away
> in a prison unless Jolly
> came in peaceful, empty hands,
> to pay the price for all his vengeance.
> Manse Jolly had other plans.

> He saddled up old Dixie
> in '66 one Sunday morn,
> about the time the Yankees
> heard their get-up bugler horn;

he galloped the streets on Dixie,
pistol in every hand.
Manse Jolly didn't stop shooting
'til there was no one left to stand.

Then Jolly kept on riding
to Texas and a farm.
Lived there more years a Christian,
doing no one any harm.
Died on Dixie in swollen waters
brought on by a flood.
His grave's in Milam County,
epitaph written in blood.

There's a lesson here for learning,
about vengeance and its price.
There's a sermon for some preacher
who would put your soul on ice.
But the thing about Manse Jolly—
he did just what he meant,
and if that wasn't Christian,
it was sure Old Testament.

The Haunting War

Put to music by Bill and Carla Coleman for their two-person drama and CD of the same name.

> When child is lost to mother,
>
> or brother lost to brother,
>
> there is pain unlike any other
>
> that haunts for years to come.
>
> When that pain is shared by nations
>
> in a million permutations
>
> that burden generations,
>
> we've just touched what war has done.

Chorus:

> It still echoes down the ages,
>
> past empty rooms and cages;
>
> grief in all its crushing stages.
>
> Close the wound and hide the scar.
>
> But some scars do not stay hidden,
>
> be they distant and unbidden.
>
> Healing seems as though forbidden
>
> by this haunting, haunting war.

As it haunted Lee and Lincoln,
it still colors people's thinking,
and though its memory is shrinking,
its effects stay near at hand.
It was the nightmare of our nation,
worse than all imagination,
defying graveyard and cremation,
it still stalks across our land.

Thousands bled and died to end it,
but ending could not mend it,
and though we try to comprehend it,
it's too much for us to ken.
A war today must pale beside it,
though it crushes those inside it.
We must unite and all decide it
will never happen here again.

The Last Roses

Put to music by Bill Coleman and included in his and Carla's CD of the same name in 2001.

We were the flower,

the light and the power;

the object of everything dear.

If asked we'd have told

that we'd never grow old,

but friends, just look at us here.

Where did time go?

When did blond become snow?

When did youth slip away from our lives?

Are we no long those

whom our countrymen chose

to ensure that our nation would thrive?

Has it been fifty years

since we marched to their cheers

and vowed we would conquer or die?

We who once were so fine

are the last on the vine—

the last roses; the summer's last sigh.

We thought there'd be more

than that horrible war

around which our lives would revolve,

but now as ends near,

we see nothing's as dear

of all in which we've been involved.

So pull those chairs near

so we can all of us hear,

and let's re-tell the tales we love best.

Let's stir up what fire

hasn't already expired.

These old roses will soon be at rest

Rebel Yell

None of us have heard it.
None of us ever will.
There's no one left who can give it,
tho' you may hear its echo still.
You may hear it near Manassas,
and down around Gaines Mill.
In December it echoes on Mayre's Heights,
and in May around Chancellorsville.

It's the "pibroch of southern fealty."
It's a Commanche brave's battle cry.
It's an English huntsman's call the hounds.
It's a farmer's call to the sty.
It's a high-pitched trilling falsetto.
It's the yip of a dog in flight.
It's the scream of a wounded panther.
It's the shriek of the wind in the night.

It was yelled when the boys flushed a rabbit.
It was passed man to man in the ranks.
It was cheered when they saw their leaders.
It was screamed when they whipped the Yanks.
But none of us ever will hear it,
tho' some folks mimic it well.
No soul alive and truly describe
the sound of the Rebel Yell

J.E.B.

*Put to music by Bill Coleman and included it in his and
Carla's Chantilly Remembrance CD (1998).*

> He was movement, excitement, baritone song,
>
> A pinpoint in time, which dazzled, long gone.
>
> Boots to the thigh,
>
> sword at the waist,
>
> a sparkling blue eye,
>
> a life lived in haste.
>
> Plume on the hat brim, spur made of gold;
>
> those who die youthful never grow old.
>
> He who died youthful,
>
> but lived every hour,
>
> God granted glory—
>
> the cavalier flower.
>
> Who promised his mother
>
> no liquor he'd drink,
>
> who from God and no other
>
> he ever did shrink,
>
> who filled winds with laughter
>
> and banjo's gay sound,
>
> whom thousands rode after
>
> and he McClellan rode round.

Such auburn-haired Beauty
we'll not see again;
a man who did duty
from beginning to end.
No tribute can cover
his life's flow and ebb.
It's enough there's no other
than the cavalier, JEB.

Jackson, or a Rabbit

Put to music by Bill Coleman and included in the CD
"Chantilly Remembrance" (1998).

We rose with the moon, in the road before two,
doin' it Old Jack's way.
Traveling light, no tents or packs.
we'll march 40 miles today.

We're stealing a march on Mister John Pope,
or maybe it's Banks tonight.
Old Jack knows, but we don't ask.
We've decided his judgment's all right.

Kyd Douglass came by with some order of
Jack's,

something short and straight to the point.

We'll do it, by God, whatever it is!

We'll do it or die if we don't.

Things have gotten right thin this last year or
so—

our rations, our looks, and our ranks—

but those of left are hell in fight.

For details, just ask Mr. Banks.

Sometimes when we're marching, the Yell's
taken up

from the front of the column on back,

and before it gets to you, comes a murmur
along—

"It's a rabbit, or else it's old Jack!"

'Cause when we see either, there's no way to
stifle

that wonderful, wild Rebel noise.

There's a lot we may lose but it's worth it to
say,

"We were known as Old Stonewall's boys."

My Grandfather's Song

Put to music by Bill Coleman and included in the CD "Chantilly Remembrance" (1998).

The Depression saw my childhood days
and home my only palace,
with my grandfather of ninety years,
the past his only solace.
The stories of his early life
I heard but could not follow,
but they were all he gave to me
to take to my tomorrow.

He'd pluck the strings of his banjo
and sing a faltering ballad
from another time, so real to him
now lost and barely hallowed,
of hopes he had which were denied
to him and his young nation;
my grandfather—an old rebel—
alone with his frustration.

He'd speak of places strange to me,
of skirmishes and fighting,

of Kelly's Ford and Fleetwood Hill
and days of endless riding.
I listened as a child will do,
tho' never comprehending,
and wondered why each tale he told
was wistful in its ending.

One night when I was nearly nine
he walked out to our stable,
though he'd not been out of bed for weeks,
not even to the table.
He climbed a horse and rode it to
a pasture of our neighbor's,
and died alone in his old gray coat
clutching his rusty saber.

Today I often think of him
and what he tried to show me.
I wonder if I'll be the same
and will have a child who knows me.
And some nights when I'm all alone,
I hear the creak of saddles.
It's Grandfather and Stuart's men,
Returning from their battles.

Closing

Body of Work

When the last of the feast has simmered away

and the depth of the cauldron is known,

the congeal at the bottom is the work of one's
life,

words, structures, art, music, and bone.

Some leavings are refuse, scraps, meaningless
rhyme,

a few diamonds, some silver, some wood.

Some will sink into other simmering pots,

slowly cook down, then vanish for good.

These are my leavings, the grease at the base

of a vessel that soon will be gone.

Do with them however they best mix with
yours;

enjoy them, ignore them, move on.